Farm Animals

Horses

Rachael Bell

Heinemann Library
Chicago, Illinois

©2000 Reed Educational & Professional Publishing
Published by Heinemann Library,
an imprint of Reed Educational & Professional Publishing,
Chicago, IL

Customer Service 888-454-2279

Designed by AMR
Originated by Ambassador Litho
Printed in China

07 06
10 9 8 7 6 5

Library of Congress Cataloging-in-Publication Data
Bell, Rachael.
    Horses / Rachael Bell.
        p. cm. – (Farm animals)
    Includes bibliographical references (p.)and index.
    Summary: Introduces this familiar farm animal, exploring birth, growth, living conditions, and uses of the horse.
    ISBN 1-57572-531-2 (lib. bdg.)   ISBN 1-58810-365-X (pbk. bdg.)
    1. Horses--Juvenile literature. [1. Horses.] I. Title.
SF 302 .B45 2000
636.1--dc21   99-044184
                                                                    CIP

Acknowledgments
The Publishers would like to thank the following for permission to reproduce photographs:
Bruce Coleman, pp. 6, 10; FLPA, p. 5; Foto Natura/Images of Nature/FLPA/J. Neukamof, p. 13; Hutchison Library/Robert Francis, p. 25; Images of Nature/FLPA/Mark Newman, pp. 5, 16, 22; Images of Nature/FLPA/Chris Newton, p. 17; Images of Nature/FLPA/Hans Dieter Brandl, p. 19; Images of Nature/FLPA/M. J. Thomas, p. 24; Bob Langrish, pp. 4, 14, 28; Only Horses Picture Library, pp. 8, 9, 11, 12, 15, 18, 20, 23, 26; Photo Disc, p. 29; Lynn M. Stone, pp. 21, 27; Tony Stone Images/Rainer Grosskopf, p. 7.

Cover photograph reproduced with permission of Heather Angel.

Our thanks to the American Farm Bureau Federation for their comments in the preparation of this book.

Every effort has been made to contact copyright holders of any material reproduced in this book. Any omissions will be rectified in subsequent printings if notice is given to the Publisher.

Some words are shown in bold, **like this.** You can find out what they mean by looking in the glossary.

Contents

Horse Relatives

Horses come in many different colors and sizes. They have long hair over their eyes, down their neck, and in their tail. Their **coat** is made of shorter hair.

There are wild horses in some parts of the world. Wild horses live in **herds**. Within the herd, the horses stay in small groups.

Welcome to the Farm

Farmers often **raise** more than one kind of animal. On this farm, there are horses and cows.

6

The land on the farm is used for
pasture. Grass grows in all the
fields. The horses and cows have
plenty of space to **graze**.

Meet the Horses

forelock

tail

hoof

The female horse is called a mare. Mares have one baby at a time. The babies are usually born in the spring.

ear

crest

withers

nose

mane

The male horse is called a stallion.
Stallions have thicker necks than
mares. All horses have a good sense
of smell and hearing.

Meet the Baby Horse

A newborn baby horse is called a foal.
A male is called a colt. A female is
called a filly. Foals stay with their
mother for about six months.

Foals can stand almost as soon as they are born. Their legs seem very long at first. Foals play and run a lot.

Where Do Horses Live?

The horses on this farm stay in
stables in the winter. They go
out once a day for exercise.
In the summer, they spend most
of their days out in the **pasture.**

Each **stall** has a deep layer of **bedding**. The bedding is usually made from wood shavings or straw. There is a rack of **hay** for the horses to eat.

What Do Horses Eat?

Horses eat at least three times a day. They eat grass, **grain,** and **hay.** They need plenty of clean water to drink.

Horses have long front teeth with a very flat edge. They use these teeth to cut the grass. Then they chew the grass with their back teeth and swallow it.

Staying Healthy

Horses need plenty of exercise to stay healthy. They like running and **prancing** around together outside. Horses like being with people, too.

Horses are careful about what they eat. They like clean grass. They leave the weeds. Horses also lick dirt and stones to get **minerals**.

How Do Horses Sleep?

At night, horses usually lie down on one side. If they are outside, they find a **sheltered** area. Every few hours, they wake up to eat or drink.

18

During the day, horses can sleep standing up. They lower their head and bend a **hind foot** to rest it. Horses wake easily if something bothers them.

19

Raising Horses

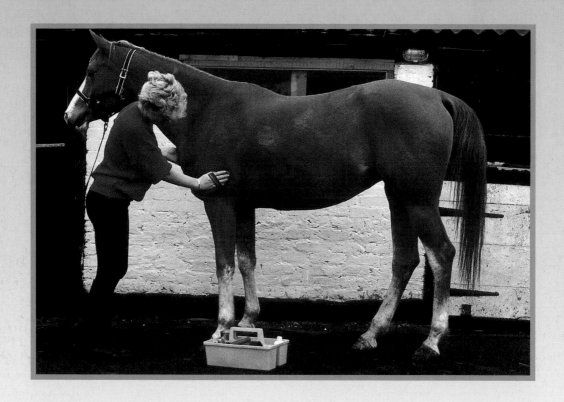

Farmers take good care of their horses. They **groom** the horses by brushing their coats, manes, and tails.

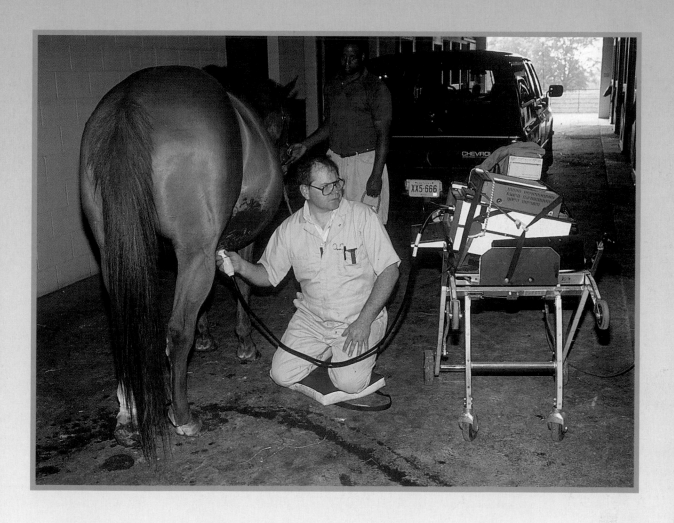

A **veterinarian** gives the horses a checkup two times each year. Horses get **vaccinations** to protect against diseases. Horses wear metal shoes that protect their **hooves.**

How Are Horses Used?

The horses on some farms are kept because their owners enjoy riding them. Some horses are used to teach children how to ride.

Other farms **raise** horses for sports such as **show-jumping,** racing, or polo. Polo is like hockey played on horseback.

More Horse Farms

Horses are very strong and **intelligent**. In many countries, people use horses to pull heavy loads or farm equipment.

Some people use horses to round up
cattle. The riders and horses keep
the cattle together as they move them
from place to place.

Special Stables

The police have large **stables** of horses. The horses are specially trained so they are not frightened by traffic or large crowds of people.

Some farms that raise race horses
are called stables. The stallions and
mares on these farms cost thousands
of dollars.

27

Fact File

A horse's height is measured in hands. A hand is about as long as the distance across the back of an adult's hand.

One of the largest horses is called the shire horse. A shire horse stands about as tall as an adult. The Falabella is the smallest horse. It comes from **South America.** It is often called a toy horse.

Horse hair is sometimes used in furniture and mattresses. It is also used to make the bows of some musical instruments.

bow

horse hair

Only ostriches have larger eyes than horses. A horse can look in two different directions at once, because its eyes can move separately.

When horses point their ears ahead, it means that they are curious about something that is in front of them. When horses lay their ears against their head, they are angry.

Glossary

bedding straw or tiny pieces of shaved wood spread over the floor of a horse's stall

cattle baby and adult cows and bulls

forelock hair that grows on the front of a horse's head

grain plant such as corn or wheat

graze to eat grass in fields

groom to clean

hay cut and dried grass

herd name for a group of horses

hind foot back foot

hoof (more than one are called hooves) horse's foot

intelligent smart

mineral substance found in the earth that animals and plants need to stay healthy

pasture fields of grass for animals to eat

prancing jumping and running that horses do for pleasure

raise to feed and take care of animals or young children

sheltered safe from bad weather

show-jumping competition in which riders on horseback jump over objects such as fences or hedges

South America continent on which countries such as Argentina, Brazil, and Peru are located

stables special buildings where horses are kept

stall small space in a barn where an animal is kept

vaccination medicine that is put into the body with a needle—also called a shot

veterinarian doctor for animals

withers shoulders of a horse

More Books to Read

Royston, Angela. *Horses and Ponies.* Des Plaines, Ill.: Heinemann Library, 1997.

Frisch, Carlienne. *Horses.* Vero Beach, Fla.: Rourke Publications, Inc., 1997. An older reader can help you with this book.

Parker, Jane. *Fantastic Book of Horses.* Danbury, Conn.: Millbrook Press, Inc., 1998. An older reader can help you with this book.

Index